HINTS ON HOME BREWING

by C. J. J. BERRY

(*Editor, "The Amateur Winemaker"*)

———

A concise guide to the making of all types of homebrew similar to mild, bitter and brown ales, stout, milk stout, strong stout, and lager, from malt, malt extract, dried malt extract, and grains.

———

THIRTIETH IMPRESSION 1984

———

SBN 900841 20 6

We would like to acknowledge the great help which we have had in preparing this booklet from Mr. Humfrey Wakefield, Mr. Hugh Semple, Mr. C. Wormwell, and many other "brewing" friends.

An "Amateur Winemaker" Publication

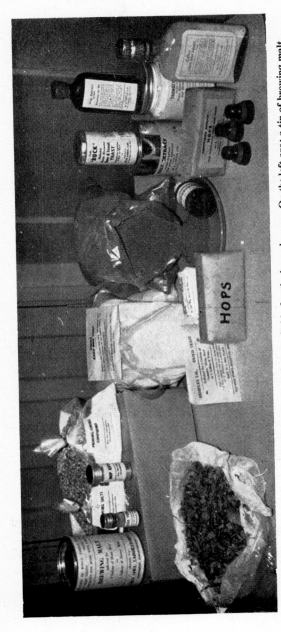

Examples of some of the specialised ingredients now available for the home brewer. On the left are: a tin of brewing malt, lager yeast, brewing salts, hop extracts, fining compound and (foreground) hops. Behind them is a dish of barley malted at home. In the centre, in the two large polythene bags, are samples of dried malt extract, pale and dark, packeted yeasts, brewing salts, compressed hops and hop extract; on the right are Buck yeast, hop extract, malt extract, compressed hops, beer finings, and new stoppers to replace damaged ones, or those the rubber rings of which have perished.

Homebrew

IT is perfectly possible for anyone, with very little equipment indeed, to make an excellent, nourishing and impressive homebrew. It will not be exactly the same as the beers and stouts to be obtained at your "local," but can be just as good, and even stronger.

For 80 years it was necessary to have a licence for home brewing and perhaps to pay duty upon the beer produced, but in his Budget of April 3, 1963, the Chancellor of the Exchequer, Mr. Reginald Maudling (Upon Whom May Blessings Descend), abolished this tiresome legislation. Consequently as a home brewer, **you are now free to brew as much beer as you please,** of any strength, and the only restriction which must be observed is that not a drop of it must be SOLD.

Commercial ales and beers—ale once had no hops, but now there is virtually no distinction—are malt liquors, and homebrew is made on the same principle. The starch in the malt is converted to sugar, which is then fermented by yeast half (by weight) to alcohol and half to carbon dioxide, the gas which gives the sparkle and head.

Quality and strength:

MOST home brewers in their early days fall into the error of trying to brew as strong a beer as possible—("got a kick like a mule!"). This, it should be pointed out, is not difficult, for yeast will ferment up to 15% if sufficient sugar is added. But a *beer* of that strength would be of little use, because it could not be drunk in quantity. What is far more difficult to attain is *quality*, in flavour, clarity, and head, and you will do far better to concentrate throughout on these. For strong beers, sugar and malt *together* should weigh 2 lbs. per gallon, for medium beers 1 lb.

In all our recipes American readers should substitute **5** American gallons for **4** English gallons (see "Brewing Vocabulary"). The pound is the same in both countries.

Ingredients

MALT HOPS SUGAR YEAST WATER

These are the basic ingredients, and many changes can be rung upon them to produce widely varying brews. Principles to remember: 1. The more malt, the more body, flavour and strength
2. The more body, the more bitterness required
3. The more hops, the greater the bitterness.
4. The more sugar, the greater the strength.

Malt:

CAN be bought in three ways, as (*a*) **barley,** which must be germinated, dried, crushed and mashed in hot water at home to convert its starch into sugar, (*b*) **grain malt,** which will need to be mashed, and (*c*) **malt extract.** The first process is both tricky and tedious, the second is highly effective but rather expensive, and for homebrew the use of malt extract, either liquid or dried, is far and away the best, because it has merely to be dissolved in the hot, hopped water, cooled and fermented. The flavour of the beer depends largely on the quality of the malt or extract used, so buy only the best from a reliable home brew supplier. If you buy extract from a chemist, avoid the type which includes cod liver oil! It is usually sold in 1lb., 2lb., or 14lb. jars or tins. One can obtain a liquid black caramelised extract for making "stout." Extract can also be purchased in dry powder form, equally good, and pleasanter to handle. When using malt extract you can greatly improve the flavour of the brew by boiling 1lb. crystal malt in the wort with the hops. For "stout" use some dark malt grain in the same way.

Grain malt, like coffee, can be roasted light or dark; pale malt is best for light or bitter beers, black malt for dark homebrew of stout quality, and patent black malt for black homebrew, the equivalent of extra stout. Or, if using ordinary malt extract for a "stout," you can boil about ¼lb. of patent black malt grain per gallon with the hops to give you the requisite darker colour.

Hops:

HOPS impart the characteristic bitterness to beer and improve its keeping qualities. Stale hops are useless, and again, it pays to buy from a specialist supplier. Hops are normally sold in 8 oz. packets and on an average 1 oz. (a fistful) will be needed per gallon, but more in stronger, heavier beers. They are best boiled in some or all of the water, in a muslin hop bag with a long string. They can then be easily agitated in the water, and removed when infusion is complete. Squeeze the bag *lightly* when it is cool enough. A few dry hops added to the "wort," (as the brew is called when ready for fermenting) will improve the flavour and replace volatile aromas lost during boiling. One can also buy hop extract, which is merely added direct to the wort, again providing a useful "short cut." Other herbs can be used instead of hops, as explained under "Other Ingredients."

4

Yeast:

A GENUINE brewer's ale or lager yeast, which will give a firm sediment, is essential. Baker's yeast will make a tolerable beer but often imparts a bakehouse mustiness, and at the least vibration or movement of the bottle will rise and cloud the homebrew. With your yeast use some form of yeast nutrient or corn salts to give it a boost and make it fully effective.

Sugar:

ORDINARY household sugar, whether cane or beet, is quite satisfactory; invert sugar, as used in breweries, is better since it ferments more readily and completely. Generally speaking, at least 1 lb. of sugar ($1\frac{1}{4}$ lb. invert) to the gallon will be necessary. If you wish to invert your own boil 8 lb. ordinary household sugar gently in two pints of water with half a teaspoonful of citric or tartaric acid, for half an hour, stirring occasionally. Cool, and add about 2 pints of water to give a total volume of exactly 1 gallon. One pint of this syrup contains 1 lb. of invert sugar.

COLOURING

Brown and **Demerara** sugar will impart some colour to your homebrew, but will also affect taste, and colouring is best done by the use of darker or black malts, by the use of stout extract, or by careful additions to the wort of caramel (bought as liquid gravy browning!). A little experiment will soon produce the exact colouring you desire; a dessertspoonful to five gallons will usually produce a light brown beer. It should be added to the water and boiled with the hops; added later it does not always remain in solution.

For sweetening a stout, use **lactose**, which will not ferment, so there is no fear of exploding bottles. It needs usually to be added at the rate of 4 oz. to the gallon.

Part of the total sugar can be replaced by an equal quantity of honey, taking care to boil the honey with the hops.

Water:

HARD water is required for pale and bitter beers, soft water for "milds" and "stouts." Water can be hardened by the use of plaster of Paris, or gypsum (calcium sulphate) at the rate of up to 1 level teaspoon per gallon, and softened by boiling, though a water softener is an obvious advantage. The addition of 1 teaspoon of salt to 4 gallons will also help. One can buy from homebrew firms for a few pence "water treatments" to achieve any desired result. Such water treatments brings out the full flavour of malt and hops and should be done during the initial boiling.

Other ingredients:

VARIOUS **grains** can be utilised to supply extra starch/sugar—maize, oats, rye, rice—and are boiled with the hops. Even bran will make a good beer. Other **herbs** can be used with or instead of hops—nettles, sage, rue, spruce oil, (a few drops per gallon), dandelion, wormwood, or burdock.

Aids to good fermentation and results are:

(1) a few drops of lemon juice.
(2) $\frac{1}{4}$ teaspoon ammonium phosphate or any proprietary yeast nutrient as directed.
(3) a pinch of grape tannin or a tablespoon of strong stewed tea per gallon, to help clarification.
(4) a pinch of Epsom salts **or** a proprietary water treatment
(5) $\frac{1}{2}$ teaspoon salt per gallon, to go in with hops when simmering.
(6) colouring: stout extract or caramel gravy browning.

Where to purchase: The firms in our list of suppliers are all entirely reliable and can supply all your brewing requirements.

Equipment:

NO need for expensive equipment, until you get *really* bitten by the bug! Most of the things you need you will already have at home, such as a 2-gallon polythene bucket, and a 1-gallon saucepan to use as a measure. But try to obtain one really large container, enough to hold 5-7 gallons; a polythene dustbin costing about £1 is ideal; light, easily-cleaned, and non-toxic. Avoid metal containers for fermenting, since they may be attacked by the nutrient acid, but almost any metal boiler will do for beer, since no acid is involved at the boiling stage. Five-gallon glass carboys can often be "acquired," and, fitted with a fermentation lock, are excellent for brewing. Try to obtain as large a boiling vessel as possible, one holding at least three gallons, and if you can run to an electric or gas wash-boiler you can brew with the minimum difficulty. Other useful items: a 50-watt immersion heater; 4-gallon tap-jars for making sparkling beer; quart beer bottles; a rubber tube for siphoning; a hydrometer; a hop bag; a nylon strainer; a thermometer (5 degrees to boiling point). **Casks** are of little use in brewing: they are difficult to keep "sweet" and, even worse, after three or four days the homebrew is "flat." Stone tap-jars are infinitely preferable. Your equipment can be as simple or as fanatically precise as *you* decide. You could brew in a bathtub, but you would probably have to drink alone!

Items of equipment for conveniently brewing 4 gallons at a time: A three-gallon boiler a "dixie" like this is quite suitable, since only two of the four gallons need be boiled, the remaining water can be added cold), a 5-gallon polythene dustbin for fermenting, a large nylon sieve for straining, a rubber tube for siphoning, polythene funnels, and a thermometer. The large quart flagons with screw stoppers are virtually indispensable in making an attractive, sparkling beer with a good "head," and you will need 16 or 17 (buy them from an off-licence at 10p each) and one or two smaller ones for odd quantities. Check that they are not chipped or cracked (and therefore weakened) and that the rubber washers on the stoppers are not perished. Finally, a hydrometer and jar are an additional insurance against explosions.

Using the hydrometer

A HYDROMETER is a worthwhile investment, for it will tell you how a fermentation is progressing, when it is safe to bottle, and how strong your finished beer is. Strong beers start with gravities of 80°-90° end at 5°-10°, alcohol 8% or 9%; medium beers start at about 45°, end round about zero, alcohol 5% or so.

You will need a hydrometer giving Specific Gravity readings including the range 1000 to 1100.

The Hydrometer (contd.)

A typical record of the progress of a fermentation:—

Initial S.G. of wort before adding yeast				1040
S.G. after 1 day	..	..	..	1034
„ 2 days	..	..	..	1023
„ 3 days	..	..	..	1011
„ 4 days	..	..	..	1006
„ 5 days	..	..	..	1003
,, 6 days	..	..	..	1001
„ 7 days	..	..	..	1000

At this stage the homebrew may be bottled, enough sugar being added to each bottle to raise the S.G. **to not above 1010.** This will "prime" sufficiently; more may cause burst bottles, and will certainly give undue sediment

It cannot be over-emphasised that the few pence a hydrometer costs are well spent indeed, for by checking the S.G. with it before you bottle you can remove any risk. For light beers the S.G. must be 1005 or below, for heavy beers 1010 or below.

To calculate the strength of your brew, take the last S.G. from the first, (omit any "decimal point") and divide the answer by 7.36. Thus:—

Initial S.G.	..	1040
Final S.G.	..	1000
Difference		40

$$40 \div 7.36 = 5.4\%$$

So this particular brew is nearly $5\frac{1}{2}\%$ alcohol by volume. If you wish your next brew stronger, add more sugar; weaker, use less sugar.

Cleanliness

... is absolutely essential throughout. Wild yeasts and other bacteria must be kept at bay, and all equipment must be regularly sterilised with boiling water or, if glass, with sodium metabisulphite (or potassium metabisulphite) solution (4 oz. in 1 gallon of water). Clean all vessels immediately after use, and leave your carboy and jars partly filled with a weak sulphite solution, and corked, when not in use. Dissolve a tiny amount of metabisulphite in the water in the U-bend of your fermentation lock.

Method using malt extract

THIS is a handy and reliable range of home-brews based on malt extract devised by Mr. Humfrey Wakefield:—

TO MAKE 5 GALLONS

Recipe	1	2	3	4
Alcohol	3%	5%	7%	9%
Gravity at Start	30	45	60	80
Gravity at Finish	–2	0	5	9
Gallons Water	5	5	5	5
lbs. sugar	3	4	5	6
lbs. Malt Extract	1	2	3	4
Herbs	1 pkt. 'Botanical Beer" Herbs H & H 28	2 oz. Hops 2 oz. Spruce Extract	4-6 oz. Hops	6-8 oz. Hops
Price per pint	2p	2½p	3p	4p
Days to clear	7	14	21	28
Keeps for	Weeks	'Months	Months	Years

Use also in each case: 1 Pkt. Dried Yeast,
1 Pkt. Yeast Food,
2 teaspoon salt, **or** water treatment as in-structed,
Juice of one lemon.

For Stout: Boil up ½ lb. patent black malt grains and 4 oz. flaked barley with the hops, in Recipe 3 or 4.

The procedure

MALT extract, as already pointed out, is the easiest ingredient to use because excellent results can be obtained from a "cold brew," i.e. one where it is unnecessary to boil the whole of the wort. Some experienced brewers, however, *do* prefer to boil the whole wort to ensure its complete sterility, and if you have a large enough boiler there is no reason why all the ingredients should not be put in it and boiled together.

Otherwise bring to the boil as much water as your boiler will take, say two or three gallons (after room has been left for the hops and the vigour of the boiling). Add the hops—it is a good idea to put them in a muslin bag—salt, and, if you are using it, the "extra" grain malt and caramel colouring. Simmer for 45 minutes; add a few **extra** hops in the last five minutes. Put the sugar and malt extract into the fermenting vessel; the malt will pour more easily if the jars are stood in hot water for 10 minutes first, and the sticky ribbon of malt can best be handled by dipping the free hand in a bowl of cold water to prevent its adhering to the fingers. Strain the near-boiling infusion on to the malt and sugar. (If using a carboy, partly fill it with cold water first, and use a plastic funnel, to avoid cracking it). Make up with cold or warm water to the required final volume, and add citric acid, and water treatment. Leave enough room for the frothing which will take place. Allow to cool to 70°F. and then add yeast and nutrient.

Fermentation:

IF possible introduce yeast at 70°F. or thereabouts. Ferment for 3-7 days at a temperature of about 65°F., and keep temperature as constant as possible, or varying lengths of fermentation will result. The lower the temperature, the slower the ferment, the higher the temperature (below, say, 75) the faster the ferment. A consistent temperature is more important than a high one, so keep the fermentation vessel away from draughts, and cover with blanket if necessary. If room temperature is low, use a small immersion heater coupled to a thermostat. Check occasionally with a thermometer, **and do not let temperature exceed 80°F., or yeast may be killed.**

If using an open crock or polythene dustbin, cover with a sheet of stout polythene secured by elastic; if using a carboy, fit a fermentation lock. If covered only with a blanket, so that more air gains access, more yeast will form on the surface, necessitating daily skimming. The first "head" or froth which forms on the brew evidently carries up with it much of the aromatic oils of the hops. for if you taste it you will see that it has a pronounced bitterness that lingers unpleasantly in the back of the throat, and your beer may later have this quality, a stronger bitterness than the one we seek, and tasted further back in the throat. If you are reluctant to throw away the skimmed foam, (and it does seem a shame) leave it in the brew, but in that case cut down drastically on the hops.

If despite your precautions, you eventually produce a beer which is too bitter for your taste, the bitterness can be masked by the use of liquorice. Dissolve a 5p stick in a saucepan over the stove, with a little hot water, and add the resulting syrup to your brew "to taste," that is, a little at a time, until it seems to you that it has done the trick.

With a "closed" fermentation and a "bottom" yeast (one which works from the bottom) skimming is unnecessary. After the initial frothing and the formation of the exciting "corona," or ring, the "head" may turn a dirty brown. Do not worry about this, all is in order.

With strong beers, add half the sugar at the outset, the remainder after three days, stirring thoroughly; if all the sugar is used at the outset they may "stick" at 1020 or so.

When the surface of the beer begins to clear, but bubbles collect in a ring in the centre (or when the S.G. is below 1010, and as near as possible to 1000) you can bottle.

Priming — for head and sparkle

IF your beer is put straight into bottles or tap jars at this stage, it will have little of that so-desirable head and sparkle, and will be "draught" in character. To obtain the sparkle it is necessary to add **1 level teaspoonful of sugar** to each quart beer bottle, which is enough to start a slight fermentation in the bottle, and give the drink a good sparkle. **DO NOT EXCEED THIS QUANTITY,** or you will have a burst bottle or, when the stopper is unscrewed, a Vesuvius of foam.

Bottling

BEER is best kept in **brown** bottles to avoid its being affected by light.

Wash your bottles under the tap vigorously, then sterilise each one with a stock solution made by dissolving $\frac{1}{4}$ lb. of potassium metabisulphite in a quart of hot water. (This can be kept in a screw-stopper flagon and used as required). Pour two ounces of the solution into the first bottle, swirl it around so that it contacts every part of the interior, and then, using a funnel, transfer it to the next bottle, until all have been done. Return the solution to its flagon. Give all the bottles a quick rinse, and dip the stoppers in the sulphite before rinsing them likewise.

Stand the bottles at a lower level than the brew vessel, perhaps in a crate, and, using a siphon, so as not to disturb the sediment, fill them one by one. Fill only to the shoulder, or your beer may foam too vigorously when unstoppered. Use a funnel and prime each bottle with one level teaspoon of castor sugar. Wet the stoppers and screw down **hard.** Use a clip on your siphon tube so that you can easily stop the flow if you want to stop part-way through bottling. Keep the bottles in a reasonably warm place (about 65°F.) for two days, then move into a cooler one, such as the larder to assist clarification.

Twenty-four hours after bottling, check that stoppers are still tight; they may have loosened, in which case your beer will go flat.

The brewing process

1

Making 4 GALLONS OF "BERRYBREW," a strong bitter. Ingredients (l. to r., back): 1 dessertspoonful caramel gravy browning, (Crosse & Blackwell's), 2 lb. sugar, 1 teaspoon citric acid, 4lb. malt extract; (front) yeast nutrient, yeast, 4oz. hops, 2 teaspoons salt 4 gallons water.

2

Put malt extract, hops, salt & caramel colouring into some or all of the water (here two gallons are used), but make sure you have a few hops to add later. Bring to boil. Simmer for 40 minutes.
Add a few loose hops, simmer for further five minutes

n six easy stages

3 >

Put the sugar into the fermentation vessel. Strain the hopped wort on to it. Stir well to dissolve. Add acid, and any "extras" such as water treatment. Make up to the desired quantity with the remainder of the water, cold. (If using carboy for fermentation, prepare the wort in another open vessel and then pour into carboy).

4 >

Allow to cool to 70°F., add yeast and nutrient Use proprietary yeasts in quantities advised by suppliers. With baker's yeast use 2 oz., creamed in some of the wort; with granulated yeast, use 3 level teaspoons.

◄5

Close vessel with poly
thene sheet or, if car
boy, with air lock. Fer
mentation should b
visible after 36 hour
complete in 10 day

6►

Siphon into bottles;
prime each with level
teaspoon of sugar;
screw down stoppers;
store in cool, dark
place.

Sediment:

NOTE that **there is bound to be some yeast sediment in the bottle finally,** because of that secondary fermentation in the bottle. This is unavoidable, and really does not matter because (*a*) if the homebrew is steadily and carefully poured, very little of it will be clouded, (*b*) you can afford to waste a little, since homebrew is so cheap, and (*c*) if you drink the dregs anyway, yeast is good for you. You can, of course, protect your aesthetic sensibilities by using a pewter tankard!

Using tap jars:

FILL only to the shoulder (this takes 4 gallons) to allow space for the considerable gas pressure which will build up. Dissolve 2 lbs. sugar in 1 pint of boiling water and add **three** ounces of this syrup to the jar. With heavy or strong beers reduce the sugar to 1–1½ lb. to the pint, or you may even have a jar burst, as messy as it is dangerous. So much depends on the strength of the individual jar. Screw down the stopper and see that the tap is well hammered home. It may leak a little at first as pressure builds up but this usually stops after a few days. If a tap grows mould—and it usually will—wash it off with a strong sulphite solution (see "Cleanliness").

With DRY malt extract

IN each of these German recipes, boil the dried malt and hops in the water for half an hour. Strain into fermentation jar or jars to take 2 gallons, cool to 70°F., add yeast and nutrient, fit air lock and leave to ferment in warm room for seven to eight days. "Prime" as directed under that heading, and bottle.

Light Lager: 2½ lbs. dried Malt Extract, 2 oz. hops, 2 gallons of water, Beer Yeast.

Lager (Pilsener style): 2 lbs. dried Malt Extract 1 oz. Hops, 2 gallons water, Beer Yeast.

Lager (Munich style): 3 lbs. dried Malt Extract, ½ oz. of Caramel, 1 oz. Hops, 2 gallons water, Beer Yeast.

Dark Beer or Porter: 4 lbs, Dried Malt Extract, 1 oz. of Caramel, 2 gallons water, Beer Yeast.

Ale: 3 lbs. Dried Malt Extract, 2 gallons water, 2 oz. Hops, Beer Yeast.

Malting barley yourself:

PUT barley in a container, pour *warm* water over it, and steep for three or four days; even a week's soaking will do no harm. Drain, place the grain in a dish in a warm place (about 85°F., an airing cupboard is ideal) but keep grain moist, and turn occasionally to get even sprouting. Putting the dish inside a polythene bag will help to retain moisture, but if necessary sprinkle with tepid water. After 7–10 days, when the shoot is about two-thirds the length of the grain, dry the barley (now malt) in an oven, but do not exceed 125°F. If a dark malt is required then roast it gently to the shade desired, pale, brown dark or black. Finally, crack it with a rolling pin, but do not grind. (Do not crack black malt).

Mashing

WHETHER you have made your own malt, or whether you have purchased some, to extract all its sugar (maltose and dextrose) it must then be mashed, and here temperature control is vital.

THIS CANNOT BE OVER-EMPHASISED: The temperature of the liquor, or mashing water, should be between 145° and 155°F., and on no account should the latter figure be exceeded.

Bring just under 2 gallons of water to 150°F. in a 2-gallon polythene bucket, and scatter in 2 lbs. of malt; if other grain is mentioned in the recipe it is added at the same time. Insert a 50-watt glass immersion heater (fish-tank type), cover bucket with blanket or thick cloth to conserve heat, and leave current on for 8 hours (consumption is negligible). No thermostat is necessary; such a heater, costing only 37½p, will hold these quantities at the right temperature.

Strain the wort into a boiler, add 2 ounces hops, and make up to three or even four gallons; boil for an hour. Strain, add 2 lbs. invert sugar, cool to 75°F., add yeast, and ferment in usual way. Fermentation usually takes 3 to 4 days.

This is a typical recipe, and the others for different types of beer which follow are made in the same way.

Quantities to use

TO MAKE 4 GALLONS

THE quantities in these recipes can be varied appreciably to suit your own taste. Use good quality brewer's yeast, and invariably, a nutrient for it. (Reminder: 4 English gallons = 5 U.S. gallons).

Lager

    4 gallons water
    4 lbs. pale malt
    3 lbs. white sugar
    2 ounces hops
    Lager yeast and nutrient
    1 teaspoon each, salt and citric acid

Mild

    4 gallons water
    4 lb. crystal malt
    1 lb. flaked maize
    4 lb. dark brown sugar
    4 ounces hops
    Yeast and nutrient
    1 teaspoon each, salt and citric acid
    1 dessertspoon caramel if darker colour desired

Pale Ale

    4 gallons water
    4 lb. malt
    6 lb. sugar
    4-6 ounces hops
    Yeast and nutrient
    1 teaspoon each salt and citric acid

Brown Ale

    4 gallons water
    4 lbs. roasted malt
    2 lb. golden syrup
    2 ounces hops
    Yeast and nutrient
    2 teaspoons salt
    1 teaspoon citric acid

Stout

    4 gallons water
    2 lb. patent black malt
    2 lb. crystal malt
    2 lb. golden syrup
    2 ounces hops
    Yeast and nutrient
    2 teaspoons salt
    1 teaspoon citric acid

Milk Stout

    4 gallons water
    2 lb. patent black malt
    6 ounces flaked barley
    2 lb. glucose (powdered)
    1 packet dried brewing yeast and nutrient
    1 ounce hops
    1 teaspoon salt

Oatmeal Stout

(1) 4 gallons water
    ¾ lb. rye
    ½ lb. black malt
    ½ lb. pale malt
    6 oz. oatmeal
    2 ounces hops
    4 lbs. sugar
    1 teaspoon citric acid
    Yeast and nutrient.

(2) 4 gallons water
    2 lb. roasted malt
    2 lbs. crystal malt
    4 lb. dark brown sugar
    1 lb. flaked maize
    3 oz. hops
    Yeast and nutrient
    1 teaspoon citric acid

Serving your homebrew

KEEP your homebrew in a cool, dark place. A drop in temperature of a few degrees after bottling is the greatest single factor in natural clarification, and sunlight can affect the brew's colour. So do not store in a warm, light place; equally do not go to the other extreme and keep your homebrew in a refrigerator, or it may go cloudy. A dark cupboard or bin in a cool larder is the ideal place in the average modern home. The brew should be served cool, and lagers and very light brews may be slightly chilled. Bottles should be handled slowly and gently and every effort made to avoid disturbing any sediment; when you pour, do so smoothly and continuously and allow the homebrew to "slide" down the side of the glass or tankard, building up the head gradually. Try to serve lagers and stouts in appropriate glasses to lend them authenticity, and do not use soapy water or detergent for washing these glasses, or the head will be spoilt the next time you use them. Use instead a very weak salt or soda solution. It is best not to use a cloth for drying, and to polish glasses with one which leaves no minute threads adhering. Glasses should be stood inverted on glass or paper-lined shelves, because they quickly pick up odours. For ale-type homebrews pewter tankards are unbeatable; they look well, conceal any sediment or lack of clarity, and, above all, the drink tastes infinitely better.

These finer points will add to your own pleasure and that of your friends.

It only remains to say: "Good Health!"

BREWING VOCABULARY

ACROSPIRE:
  Shoot which grows from grain of barley during malting.

ALE:
  Formerly, unhopped beer.

BARLEY:
  Grain most commonly used for brewing.

BARM:
  Mixture of wort and yeast.

BEER:
  Hopped ale.

BOTTOMS:
  Deposit of yeasts and solids formed during fermentation.

BREWERS' GRAINS:
  The insoluble residue of malt left in mash tun after the wort has been run off.

BURNT SUGAR:
  Old name for caramel colouring: prepared from glucose.

BUSH:
  Ancient sign for an inn (hence: "Good wine needs no bush") Probably of Roman origin; a "bush" of ivy and vine leaves was the symbol of the wine-god, Bacchus.

BUSH:
  Metal liner of the bung or tap-hole of a barrel.

CARBON DIOXIDE:
  Gas given off during fermentation which gives the "head" on beer and the sparkle.

CARAMEL:
  See "Burnt Sugar."

CASKS:
  Butt, 108 gallons; Puncheon, 72 gallons; Hogshead, 54 gallons; Barrel, 36 gallons; Kilderkin, 18 gallons; Firkin, 9 gallons; Pin, 4½ gallons.

CYTASE:
  Enzyme in barley grain which dissolves the cellulose protecting the granule and allows fermentation to proceed.

DEXTRINS:
  Substances in wort, released during mashing.

DIASTASE:
  Enzyme in barley which converts starch to fermentable sugar

FERMENTATION:
  Yeast working upon a sugar solution (the wort) to produce alcohol and carbon dioxide.

FERMENTATION LOCK:
  A little gadget to protect the brew from bacterial contamination.

FININGS:
Used for removing suspended solids from cloudy beer: usually isinglass.

GALLON:
8 pints, 160 liq. oz., or 277¼ cu. inches. 1 Imperial or English gallon = 1.2 U.S. gallons. Therefore in our recipes substitute for U.S. use the following gallonage:

English	..	1	2	3	4
American	..	1¼	2½	3½	5

GILL: ¼ pint.

GOODS: *See* **GRIST**

GRIST:
Barley after it has been malted and crushed. Also called "Goods.

GREEN MALT:
Germinated barley before it is kilned.

GRIT:
Any grain, other than barley, used in brewing.

GYPSUM:
Calcium sulphate. An important constituent of water ("or liquor") if beer is to clear well.

HEAD:
The creamy foam on beer.

HEADING LIQUID:
Used for adding an artificial "head."

HOP:
The flower of the hop plant (*humulus lupulus*) used in beer for its preservative and flavouring qualities.

HOP BAG:
For infusing but keeping separate the hops in the wort.

HYDROMETER:
Instrument for measuring the sugar content of a wort and strength of finished beer. (*See First Steps in Winemaking*).

HYDROMETER JAR:
Jar in which hydrometer is floated for a reading to be taken.

KILN:
Used in malting for drying malt after its germination.

LEES: See **BOTTOMS.**

LIQUOR: In brewing—water!

LUPULIN:
Yellow powder in the hop flower containing the oils and resins which give the hop its bitterness.

MALT:
Barley which has been so treated as to convert its starch into fermentable sugar.

MALTOSE:
The fermentable sugar obtained by malting.

MASH:
Mixture of malt and hot water, or the combination of ingredients from which the beer will be made.

MASH TUB (or TUN):
Container for mash.

MILK STOUT:
Former name for a stout in which lactose (milk sugar) has been utilised.

NOGGIN:
Quarter-pint.

NUTRIENT:
Nitrogenous matter added to wort to boost the action of the yeast; yeast food.

PINT:
Imperial pint—20 liq. oz.; reputed pint—a 12oz. beer bottle.

POLISHING:
Filtering beer through asbestos to give it brilliance.

PRIMING:
Adding a small quantity of sugar to a jar or bottle of beer to cause a slight further fermentation and give it a head and sparkle.

QUART:
A quarter-gallon.

QUARTERN:
A quarter-pint.

RACK:
Siphon beer off the lees into fresh container: filling a cask.

SHIVE:
Circular wooden plug, bored centrally, used to seal a filled barrel.

SPARGING:
Spraying the floating grains with hot water during mashing, whilst the wort is drawn off from below.

SPILE:
Small wooden peg which is a close fit in the hole in the shive and is loosened to admit air and allow beer to be drawn from the barrel. Afterwards it must be pressed home again or the beer will lose condition.

STILLION:
Wooden cradle or stand for barrel.

SWEET WORT:
The wort before it is boiled and hopped.

TUN:
Name given to many vessels in a brewery (c.f. Mash Tun). Once a measure (wine): 252 gallons.

WORT:
The liquid extract ready to be fermented.

YEAST:
The fermenting agent, in brewing usually a strain of saccharomyces cerevisiae.

ESSENTIAL BOOKS FOR
WINEMAKERS AND HOMEBREWERS

"FIRST STEPS IN WINEMAKING," by C. J. J. Berry.
—still the best "rapid course"

"130 NEW WINEMAKING RECIPES," by C. J. J. Berry.
—its companion volume

"HOME BREWED BEERS & STOUTS," by C. J. J. Berry.
—the first full length book on the subject

"MAKING WINES LIKE THOSE YOU BUY," by Bryan
Acton and Peter Duncan—your own Sherry, Port, Liqueurs,
Champagne, Madeira, Hocks, etc., etc.,

"JUDGING HOME-MADE WINES," by the National
Guild of Judges.

"MAKING MEAD," by Bryan Acton and Peter Duncan—

"BREWING BETTER BEERS," by Ken Shales—

"PROGRESSIVE WINEMAKING," by Duncan & Acton

"AMATEUR WINEMAKER RECIPES," by C. J. J. Berry.

"WINEMAKING WITH CANNED & DRIED FRUIT,"
by C. J. J. Berry

"MAKING CIDER,"   by Jo Deal

"BEER KITS AND BREWING,"   by Dave Line

"WINEMAKING AND BREWING," by Drs. F. Beech &
A. Pollard